Hearty Casseroles

Baked Risotto with Asparagus, Spinach & Parmesan

- **1 tablespoon olive oil**
- **1 cup finely chopped onion**
- **1 cup arborio (risotto) rice**
- **8 cups (8 to 10 ounces) spinach leaves, torn into pieces**
- **2 cups vegetable broth**
- **¼ teaspoon salt**
- **¼ teaspoon ground nutmeg**
- **½ cup grated Parmesan cheese, divided**
- **1½ cups diagonally sliced asparagus**

1. Preheat oven to 400°F. Spray 13×9-inch baking dish with nonstick cooking spray.

2. Heat olive oil in large skillet over medium-high heat. Add onion; cook and stir 4 minutes or until tender. Add rice; stir to coat with oil.

3. Stir in spinach, a handful at a time, adding more as it wilts. Add broth, salt and nutmeg. Reduce heat and simmer 7 minutes. Stir in ¼ cup cheese.

4. Transfer to prepared baking dish. Cover tightly and bake 15 minutes.

5. Remove from oven and stir in asparagus; sprinkle with remaining ¼ cup cheese. Cover and bake 15 minutes more or until liquid is absorbed. *Makes 6 servings*

Easy Moroccan Casserole

  2 tablespoons vegetable oil
  1 pound pork stew meat, cut into 1-inch cubes
  ½ cup chopped onion
  3 tablespoons all-purpose flour
  1 can (about 14 ounces) diced tomatoes, undrained
  ¼ cup water
  1 teaspoon ground ginger
  1 teaspoon ground cumin
  1 teaspoon ground cinnamon
  ½ teaspoon sugar
  ½ teaspoon salt
  ½ teaspoon black pepper
  2 medium unpeeled red potatoes, cut into ½-inch pieces
  1 large sweet potato, peeled and cut into ½-inch pieces
  1 cup frozen lima beans, thawed and drained
  1 cup frozen cut green beans, thawed and drained
  ¾ cup sliced carrots
    Pita bread

1. Preheat oven to 325°F.

2. Heat oil in large skillet over medium-high heat. Add pork and onion; cook until pork is browned on all sides, stirring occasionally. Sprinkle flour over meat mixture. Stir until flour has absorbed pan juices. Cook 2 minutes more.

3. Stir in tomatoes with juice, water, ginger, cumin, cinnamon, sugar, salt and pepper. Transfer mixture to 2-quart casserole. Bake 30 minutes.

4. Stir in red potatoes, sweet potato, lima beans, green beans and carrots. Cover; bake 1 hour or until potatoes are tender. Serve with pita bread.   *Makes 6 servings*

Tuscan Pot Pie

¾ pound sweet or hot Italian sausage

1 jar (26 to 28 ounces) chunky vegetable or mushroom spaghetti sauce

1 can (19 ounces) cannellini beans, rinsed and drained

½ teaspoon dried thyme leaves

1½ cups (6 ounces) shredded mozzarella cheese

1 package (8 ounces) refrigerated crescent dinner rolls

1. Preheat oven to 425°F. Remove sausage from casings. Brown sausage in medium ovenproof skillet, stirring to separate meat. Drain drippings.

2. Add spaghetti sauce, beans and thyme to skillet. Simmer uncovered over medium heat 5 minutes. Remove from heat; stir in cheese.

3. Unroll crescent dough; divide into triangles. Arrange in spiral with points of dough towards center, covering sausage mixture completely. Bake 12 minutes or until crust is golden brown and meat mixture is bubbly.   *Makes 4 to 6 servings*

Note: To remove a sausage casing, use a pairing knife to slit the casing at one end. Be careful not to cut through the sausage. Grasp the cut edge and gently pull the casing away from the sausage.

Prep and Cook Time: 27 minutes

Rice & Vegetable Stuffed Squash

2 large acorn or golden acorn squash (about 1½ pounds each)
1 cup uncooked quick-cooking rice
2 cups broccoli florets, chopped
½ teaspoon black pepper
½ teaspoon salt
¼ cup chopped almonds, toasted
¾ cup shredded sharp Cheddar or smoked gouda cheese

1. Cut squash in half crosswise; scrape out and discard seeds. Trim off stems and a small portion of pointed ends to allow squash to stand when turned over. Place squash halves cut sides down on microwavable plate; microwave at HIGH 12 to 15 minutes, or until almost tender when pierced. Place squash halves in 13×9-inch baking pan, cut sides up. Cover; let stand 3 minutes or until ready to fill. Preheat oven to 375°F.

2. Meanwhile, cook rice according to package directions adding broccoli, pepper and salt during last 5 minutes of cooking. Stir in almonds.

3. Mound rice mixture into squash, overflowing into dish if necessary; sprinkle with cheese. Bake 20 to 25 minutes or until squash is tender and cheese is melted.   *Makes 4 servings*

Eggplant Parmigiana

2 eggs, beaten
¼ cup milk
   Dash garlic powder
   Dash onion powder
   Dash salt
   Dash black pepper
1 large eggplant, cut into ½-inch-thick slices
½ cup seasoned dry bread crumbs
   Vegetable oil for frying
1 jar (about 26 ounces) spaghetti sauce
4 cups (16 ounces) shredded mozzarella cheese
2½ cups (10 ounces) shredded Swiss cheese
¼ cup grated Parmesan cheese
¼ cup grated Romano cheese

1. Preheat oven to 350°F. Combine eggs, milk, garlic powder, onion powder, salt and pepper in shallow bowl. Dip eggplant into egg mixture; coat in bread crumbs.

2. Add enough oil to large skillet to cover bottom by ¼ inch. Heat over medium-high heat. Brown eggplant in batches on both sides; drain on paper towels. Cover bottom of 13×9-inch baking dish with 2 or 3 tablespoons spaghetti sauce. Layer ½ of eggplant, ½ of mozzarella cheese, ½ of Swiss cheese and ½ of remaining sauce in dish. Repeat layers. Sprinkle with Parmesan and Romano cheeses.

3. Bake 30 minutes or until heated through and cheeses are melted. *Makes 4 servings*

Macaroni & Cheese with Bacon

3 cups (8 ounces) uncooked rotini pasta
2 tablespoons butter or margarine
2 tablespoons all-purpose flour
¼ teaspoon salt
¼ teaspoon dry mustard
⅛ teaspoon black pepper
1½ cups milk
2 cups (8 ounces) shredded sharp Cheddar cheese
8 ounces bacon, crisply cooked and crumbled*
2 medium tomatoes, sliced

*1 cup cubed cooked ham can be substituted for bacon.

1. Preheat oven to 350°F. Lightly grease 1½-quart shallow casserole.

2. Cook pasta according to package directions; drain and return to saucepan.

3. Melt butter over medium-low heat in 2-quart saucepan. Whisk in flour, salt, mustard and pepper; cook and stir 1 minute. Whisk in milk. Bring to a boil over medium heat, stirring frequently. Reduce heat and simmer 2 minutes. Remove from heat. Add cheese; stir until melted.

4. Add cheese mixture and bacon to pasta; stir until well blended. Transfer to prepared casserole. Bake uncovered 20 minutes. Arrange tomato slices on casserole. Bake additional 5 to 8 minutes or until casserole is bubbly and tomatoes are hot.

Makes 4 servings

Pizza Casserole

2 cups uncooked rotini or other spiral pasta
1½ to 2 pounds ground beef
1 medium onion, chopped
   Salt and black pepper
1 can (about 15 ounces) pizza sauce
1 can (8 ounces) tomato sauce
1 can (6 ounces) tomato paste
½ teaspoon sugar
½ teaspoon garlic salt
½ teaspoon dried oregano leaves
2 cups (8 ounces) shredded mozzarella cheese
12 to 15 slices pepperoni

1. Preheat oven to 350°F. Cook rotini according to package directions. Set aside.

2. Meanwhile, cook and stir ground beef and onion in large skillet over medium-high heat until meat is no longer pink. Season with salt and pepper. Set aside.

3. Combine rotini, pizza sauce, tomato sauce, tomato paste, sugar, garlic salt and oregano in large bowl. Add beef mixture; stir until blended.

4. Place half of mixture in 3-quart casserole; top with 1 cup cheese. Repeat layers. Arrange pepperoni slices on top. Bake 25 to 30 minutes or until heated through and cheese is melted.

Makes 6 servings

Spicy Beefy Noodles

1½ **pounds ground beef**
1 **small onion, minced**
1 **small clove garlic, minced**
1 **tablespoon chili powder**
1 **teaspoon paprika**
⅛ **teaspoon** *each* **dried basil leaves, dill weed, dried thyme leaves and dried marjoram leaves**
  Salt
  Black pepper
1 **can (10 ounces) diced tomatoes with green chilies, undrained**
1 **can (8 ounces) tomato sauce**
1 **cup water**
3 **tablespoons Worcestershire sauce**
1 **package (about 10 ounces) egg noodles, cooked according to package directions**
½ **cup (2 ounces)** *each* **shredded Cheddar, mozzarella, Pepper-Jack and provolone cheeses**

1. Cook and stir ground beef, onion and garlic in large skillet over medium heat until meat is no longer pink, stirring to separate meat. Pour off drippings. Add chili powder, paprika, basil, dill, thyme and marjoram. Season with salt and pepper. Cook and stir 2 minutes.

2. Add tomatoes with juice, tomato sauce, water and Worcestershire sauce; mix well. Simmer, covered, 20 minutes.

3. In 2-quart microwavable casserole, combine meat mixture and noodles. Mix cheeses and sprinkle evenly over top.

4. Microwave at HIGH 3 minutes. Let stand 5 minutes. Microwave 3 minutes longer or until cheeses melt. *Makes 6 servings*

Shrimp Creole

2 tablespoons olive oil
1½ cups chopped green bell pepper
1 medium onion, chopped
⅔ cup chopped celery
2 cloves garlic, finely chopped
1 cup uncooked rice
1 can (about 14 ounces) diced tomatoes, drained and juice reserved
1 teaspoon dried oregano leaves
¾ teaspoon salt
½ teaspoon dried thyme leaves
2 teaspoons hot pepper sauce, or to taste
Black pepper
1 pound raw medium shrimp, peeled and deveined
1 tablespoon chopped fresh parsley (optional)

1. Preheat oven to 325°F. Heat olive oil in large skillet over medium-high heat. Add bell pepper, onion, celery and garlic; cook and stir 5 minutes or until vegetables are soft.

2. Add rice; cook and stir 5 minutes over medium heat until rice is opaque. Add tomatoes, oregano, salt, thyme, hot sauce and black pepper to skillet; stir until blended. Pour reserved tomato juice into measuring cup. Add enough water to measure 1¾ cups liquid; add to skillet. Cook and stir 2 minutes.

3. Transfer mixture to 2½-quart casserole. Stir in shrimp. Bake, covered, 55 minutes or until rice is tender and liquid is absorbed. Sprinkle with fresh parsley, if desired.   *Makes 4 to 6 servings*

Chicken, Asparagus & Mushroom Bake

1 tablespoon butter

1 tablespoon olive oil

2 boneless skinless chicken breasts (about ½ pound),
     cut into bite-size pieces

2 cloves garlic, minced

1 cup sliced mushrooms

2 cups sliced asparagus

   Black pepper

1 package (about 6 ounces) corn bread stuffing mix

¼ cup dry white wine (optional)

1 can (14½ ounces) reduced-sodium chicken broth

1 can (10½ ounces) condensed condensed cream of asparagus
     or cream of chicken soup, undiluted

1. Preheat oven to 350°F. Heat butter and oil in large skillet until butter is melted. Cook and stir chicken and garlic about 3 minutes over medium-high heat until chicken is no longer pink. Add mushrooms; cook and stir 2 minutes. Add asparagus; cook and stir about 5 minutes or until asparagus is crisp-tender. Season with pepper.

2. Transfer mixture to 2½-quart casserole or 6 small casseroles. Top with stuffing mix.

3. Add wine to skillet, if desired; cook and stir 1 minute over medium-high heat, scraping up any browned bits from bottom of skillet. Add broth and soup; cook and stir until well blended.

4. Pour broth mixture into casserole; mix well. Bake, uncovered, about 35 minutes (30 minutes for small casseroles) or until heated through and lightly browned.   *Makes 6 servings*

Saffron Chicken & Vegetables

2 tablespoons vegetable oil

6 bone-in chicken thighs, skinned

1 bag (16 ounces) frozen mixed vegetables, such as broccoli, red peppers, mushrooms and onions, thawed

1 can (14½ ounces) roasted garlic-flavored chicken broth

1 can (10¾ ounces) condensed cream of chicken soup, undiluted

1 can (10¾ ounces) condensed cream of mushroom soup, undiluted

1 package (about 8 ounces) uncooked saffron yellow rice mix with seasonings

½ cup water

½ teaspoon salt

1 teaspoon paprika (optional)

1. Preheat oven to 350°F. Spray 3-quart casserole with nonstick cooking spray; set aside. Heat oil in large skillet over medium heat. Brown chicken on both sides; drain fat.

2. Meanwhile, combine vegetables, chicken broth, soups, rice mix with seasonings, water and salt in large bowl. Place mixture in prepared casserole. Top with chicken. Sprinkle with paprika, if desired. Cover; bake 1½ hours or until chicken is no longer pink in center.   *Makes 6 servings*

Crab-Artichoke Casserole

8 ounces uncooked small shell pasta
2 tablespoons butter
6 green onions, chopped
2 tablespoons all-purpose flour
1 cup half-and-half
1 teaspoon dry mustard
½ teaspoon ground red pepper
   Salt and black pepper
½ cup (2 ounces) shredded Swiss cheese, divided
1 package (about 8 ounces) imitation crabmeat chunks
**1 can (about 14 ounces) artichoke hearts, drained and cut
   into bite-size pieces**

1. Preheat oven to 350°F. Grease 2-quart casserole. Cook pasta according to package directions; drain and set aside.

2. Melt butter in large saucepan over medium heat; add green onions. Cook and stir about 2 minutes. Add flour; cook and stir 2 minutes more. Gradually add half-and-half, whisking constantly until mixture begins to thicken. Whisk in mustard and red pepper; season to taste with salt and black pepper. Remove from heat and stir in ¼ cup cheese until melted.

3. Combine crabmeat, artichokes and pasta in casserole. Add sauce mixture and stir until blended. Top with remaining ¼ cup cheese. Bake about 40 minutes or until hot, bubbly and lightly browned. *Makes 6 servings*

Cha-Cha-Cha Casserole

1 can (about 7 ounces) whole green chilies, drained
  Nonstick cooking spray
1 pound ground turkey or chicken
1 cup chopped onion
1 tablespoon chili powder or to taste
3 cloves garlic, minced
1 teaspoon ground cumin
1 teaspoon salt (optional)
1 can (10 ounces) diced tomatoes with green chilies,
  undrained
2 cups frozen corn, thawed or canned corn, drained
1 can (16 ounces) refried beans
2 cups (8 ounces) shredded Mexican cheese blend
2 cups crushed tortilla chips
1 cup diced seeded fresh tomato
½ cup sliced green onions

1. Preheat oven to 375°F. Cut chilies in half lengthwise and arrange in single layer in 8-inch square baking dish coated with cooking spray.

2. Spray medium nonstick skillet with cooking spray. Cook and stir turkey, onion, chili powder, garlic, cumin and salt, if desired, over medium heat until turkey is no longer pink. Add canned tomatoes with juice; cook about 10 minutes or until liquid evaporates.

3. Add turkey mixture to casserole; top with corn and beans. Sprinkle with cheese and crushed chips. Bake 30 minutes; let stand 5 minutes before serving. Garnish with fresh tomato and green onions. *Makes 6 servings*

Broccoli Lasagna

2 tablespoons olive oil
1 cup thinly sliced fresh mushrooms
3 cloves garlic, minced
1 can (14½ ounces) diced tomatoes, undrained
1 can (8 ounces) tomato sauce
1 can (6 ounces) tomato paste
1 tablespoon red wine vinegar
1 teaspoon dried oregano leaves
1 teaspoon dried basil leaves
   Pinch red pepper flakes
1 cup ricotta cheese
1 cup (4 ounces) shredded mozzarella cheese, divided
¼ cups chopped fresh parsley
9 lasagna noodles, cooked and well drained
3 cups chopped broccoli (about 1 large bunch), cooked
   and well drained
1 to 2 tablespoons grated Parmesan cheese

1. Preheat oven to 350°F. Spray 8×8-inch baking pan with nonstick cooking spray. Heat oil in large saucepan over medium heat. Add mushrooms and garlic; cook and stir about 5 minutes or until mushrooms are browned and beginning to release liquid. Stir in tomatoes, tomato sauce, tomato paste, vinegar, oregano, basil and red pepper flakes. Simmer over low heat, stirring occasionally.

2. Combine ricotta, mozzarella and parsley in medium bowl; set aside. Place 3 lasagna noodles in bottom of prepared pan. Spread half ricotta mixture over noodles. Layer half of broccoli over ricotta mixture. Spoon ⅓ tomato mixture over ricotta; repeat layers. Place last 3 noodles on top; spread with remaining tomato mixture over noodles. Cover with foil sprayed with nonstick cooking spray.

3. Bake 25 minutes. Uncover; sprinkle with remaining ¼ cup mozzarella cheese and Parmesan cheese. Bake, uncovered, 10 minutes or until cheese melts. Let stand 10 minutes before serving.   *Makes 9 servings*

Salmon Casserole

    2 tablespoons margarine or butter
    2 cups mushroom slices
 1½ cups chopped carrots
    1 cup frozen peas
    1 cup chopped celery
    ½ cup chopped onion
    ½ cup chopped red bell pepper
    1 tablespoon chopped fresh parsley
    1 clove garlic, minced
    1 teaspoon salt
    ½ teaspoon black pepper
    ½ teaspoon dried basil leaves
    4 cups cooked rice
    1 can (14 ounces) red salmon, drained and flaked
    1 can (10¾ ounces) condensed cream of mushroom soup,
        undiluted
    2 cups (8 ounces) grated Cheddar or American cheese
    ½ cup sliced black olives

1. Preheat oven to 350°F. Spray 2-quart casserole with nonstick cooking spray; set aside.

2. Melt margarine in large skillet or Dutch oven over medium heat. Add mushrooms, carrots, peas, celery, onion, bell pepper, parsley, garlic, salt, black pepper and basil; cook and stir 10 minutes or until vegetables are tender. Add rice, salmon, soup and cheese; mix well.

3. Transfer to prepared casserole. Sprinkle olives over top. Bake 30 minutes or until hot and bubbly.   *Makes 8 servings*

Creamy "Crab" Fettuccine

1 pound imitation crabmeat sticks
6 ounces uncooked fettuccine
3 tablespoons margarine or butter, divided
1 small onion, chopped
2 ribs celery, chopped
$1/2$ medium red bell pepper, chopped
2 cloves garlic, minced
1 cup reduced-fat sour cream
1 cup reduced-fat mayonnaise
1 cup (4 ounces) shredded sharp Cheddar cheese
2 tablespoons chopped fresh parsley
$1/4$ teaspoon salt
$1/8$ teaspoon black pepper
$1/2$ cup cornflake crumbs
   Fresh chives (optional)

1. Preheat oven to 350°F. Spray 2-quart square baking dish with nonstick cooking spray. Cut crabmeat into bite-size pieces. Cook pasta according to package directions until al dente. Drain and set aside.

2. Meanwhile, melt 1 tablespoon margarine in large skillet over medium-high heat. Add onion, celery, bell pepper and garlic; cook and stir 2 minutes or until vegetables are tender.

3. Combine sour cream, mayonnaise, cheese, parsley, salt and black pepper in large bowl. Add crabmeat, pasta and vegetable mixture, stirring gently to combine. Pour into prepared dish.

4. Melt remaining 2 tablespoons margarine. Combine cornflake crumbs and margarine in small bowl; sprinkle evenly over casserole.

5. Bake, uncovered, 30 minutes or until hot and bubbly. Garnish with chives, if desired.   *Makes 6 servings*